# BEHOLD

## I STAND AT THE DOOR

# AND KNOCK

*With God all things are possible*

Kerry L. Batchelder

**ISBN:** 9798418857934

**Imprint:** Independently published

# ACKNOWLEDGEMENTS

To my husband Scott,
Thank you for your continual encouragement and
support as I fulfil my lifelong dream, to write.

# CONTENTS

# INTRODUCTION

The name of this book is based upon Revelations 3:20, "Behold I stand at the door and knock, if anyone hears my voice and opens the door, I will come in to him and eat with him, and he with me."

One of the poems in this book is entitled, "Behold I Stand at the Door and Knock." It conveys God's love for us as He patiently waits for us to open the door of our heart to Him.

> *"I hear a gentle knock upon the door and ignore it … Yet it comes"*
> *"Whether a pounding rap or delicate tap; I'm too busy to be bothered …Yet it comes"*

In this poem the author hears His gentle knock upon the door, but is either too busy or too preoccupied to open the door. Hearing His soft but continual knocking, she chooses to tune it out, even to the point of seeking Him, while on her knees and wondering why she is not getting answers.

When she finally opens the door she sees her Savior face to face and realizes He has been there all along, patiently waiting for her to open the door and invite Him in.

---

In this book, Kerry shares many of her most private and innermost thoughts on the subject of faith and spirituality in today's world and in her own journey through life.

Some points are merely observations, while others run deeper and have actually occurred.  Two were written for friends.  All are written with purpose.

As a Christian, she gives God full credit for the book, as it is through Him alone she is inspired to share these thoughts.

Her hopes are that you, *the reader*, may connect with her as you think of situations in your own life that may relate.

# Divine Intervention

*Contrary to all we are taught there is a power which reaches beyond the heavens creating occurrences that make no earthly sense.*

It causes plans to abruptly change with no apparent reason. It brings healing when there is no hope. It provides opportunity when we've exhausted our resources.

It causes forces to crumble, bringing the powerful to their knees. It provides a feast for the hungry and shelter for the frightened. It brings companionship to the lonely.

It is not a luxury which can be purchased or capitalized on by the wealthy. It is beyond our grasp yet available to those who trust in its power.

It does not judge and is not partial to a particular society or person. It astounds, promotes, and defies all logic.

It is Divine Intervention.

# God is Good

*God's work is never done. He does not complete a portion of what he has begun in us to suddenly wipe his hands, saying, "You are now on your own."*

He is faithful for all time. His friendship is a forever friendship, even if we choose to go our own way. He will patiently wait for us to come back to him when we have exhausted our resources. Yet He does expect us to step out in faith.

He does not set us up for failure, nor does He initiate disaster in our lives. This is the work of our adversary. He does, however work good out of a bad situation when we simply ask for His help.

He is omnipresent. In the darkest night, in the heat of battle, when we feel alone, He is there.
He speaks quietly, not forcibly, never imposing Himself upon us.

He cries with us when our hearts are broken, catching our tears in His very hands. He laughs with us when we are happy. He celebrates our accomplishments.

He is good!

# I Have a Friend

*I have a friend who is closer than a breath away, longing to talk with me about anything under the sun.*

He wants to share in good times as well as bad. He does not judge me.

He offers wise counsel in the midst of trials. He protects my family and friends. He is faithful.

My friend listens intently without interruptions and cares deeply for me. He is not pretentious or preoccupied.

I can always depend on him as he will never turn away. He helps me carry loads much too heavy to carry on my own.

He offers me a safe place to hide from the world's chaos. He provides a quiet place for me to gather my thoughts.

He is patient and kind, yet capable of fiercely defending me. His love knows no limits.

He is generous, often showering me with unexpected gifts. He makes me smile.

His name is Jesus.

# In An Instant

*When an accident took off the top of our son's
finger it saddened me.*

It occurred to me how very fragile our lives are and reminded me of how quickly life can change.

In an instant.

Then I thought of how God must have felt when He witnessed, not an accident, but the sheer brutality of mankind in the torturous death of his own son.

In an instant.

His heart must have broken as he witnessed every ounce of pain his son endured. I believe in deep remorse and bitter anger He looked away, lest he wipe out every living soul with but a single breath.

In an instant.

I believe it was at that moment, Jesus cried out with his last breath, "My God, my God why has though forsaken me!" He knew it was because his father could not endure the pain of seeing him suffer that he looked away.

For an instant.

When Jesus cried out, "It is finished," God's wrath let loose, shaking the very firmament on which we stand with a mighty earthquake. The sky went black. The inner veil of the holy of holies was ripped in two with unseen hands.

In an instant.

Through the death and resurrection of his son, Jesus Christ, we all have eternal life. Defeating death was the only way to re-establish a personal relationship between God and mankind, which man had destroyed.

In an instant.

Our lives are as a vapor in the wind. The only constant being our Father's love for us which never changes. One day He will return to bring us home.

In an instant.

# Revelation

Longing for
Conversation,
Friendship, I do not
Know.

Life
Thankless drill,
Pieces fit, others
Don't.

Age
Uphill battle,
Fiercely holding
Tight.

Drive
Escapes me,
Tired, cannot
Fight.

Denying
Wanted pleasures,
Obstacles, doors
Shut.

Taunting
World laughing,
Wanting more of
What?

Groping for
Explanations,

Something missing
Within.

Answer
Jesus calling,
Trusting in
Him.

Laughing
Crying,
Helping others
Dare.

Reflecting
Thinking backwards,
Revelation
Care.

# Gods Handiwork

*I sit motionless in the stillness of the morning looking out over the body of water they call the Big Lake. I am mesmerized by its beauty.*

Taking in the spectacular views
of the sunrise, I am in awe.
Brilliant hues explode in a breathtaking display
of vibrant color, to which there is no equal.

I hear the cry of a seagull
and look  up. I notice a flock
of white pelicans soaring in a military-like
formation above the water's surface.

The silhouette of a ship catches
my eye. It is but a tiny speck
in the large expanse, but mighty
all the same, with many stories to be told.

Fishing vessel's lines are rigged,
anticipating their daily catch.
Lures reflect the morning sun as shards
of glass beneath a spotlight.

An Eagle spreads its mighty wings;
disappearing beneath the cliff's edge.
It circles in the distance, soon to return
to the limb that holds its young.

I consider God's handiwork and
wonder how anyone can deny His  presence.
I am lost in the beauty
of His creation

# He is Our God and Father



He is goodness in its purest form.

Genuinely flawless…

Words cannot come close to defining the degree of love and devotion He has for us as His children.

He is love to the nth degree…

Consider the enormity of our passions, multiplied by the largest unit of measurement known to man…

And you will find it covers only a Planck Length of His love for us. ..

Mix that unfathomable degree of love and goodness with the power to create time and galaxies…

And you will find…

There is no limit to what God is able to accomplish, no power in heaven or earth that can stop Him. His abilities are beyond our wildest comprehension.

And to think …

He is our God and Father.

# My Sinners Prayer

*Father, may you please not hold my sins against me, but may I be cleansed through the blood and forgiveness of Jesus Christ, my Lord.*

May you please help me to be compassionate, caring, gentle and slow to anger.

May you please bless my children with good health, good morals and your favor.

May you please be with my husband, family and friends, as you watch over them.

May your power be known by all people throughout the world.
May all have the opportunity to know you as their Lord and Savior.

Lord you know my heart and the sinfulness that lies within me.
Please cleanse my heart from all unrighteousness and fill me with your Holy Spirit to overflowing.

In Jesus name I pray,

Amen

# The Dilemma of Worry

*I toss and turn, considering all possible solutions to the dilemma I now find myself in.*

Re-creating scenarios in my mind of how this situation came to be, I play it over and over in my head like a broken record. Exhausted, I fall into a restless sleep.

I wake up to the feeling of an empty pit in my stomach, once again reminded of my problem with no solution in sight.
My broken sleep offers no solace as I did not get the rest my body required. I am tired.

Focusing on the day at hand, I remain acutely aware of the problem which sits naggingly in the back of my mind.
I ignore it, knowing I must deal with it, but choosing to wait until a more opportune time.

Night settles in and I grow tired.
Welcoming the comfort of my bed, my eyes close. An hour later I am abruptly awakened to the worry which plagued me only one night before.

A prisoner of my thoughts, I cannot turn off the repeated voices that keep sounding in my brain.
I try to sleep but lie awake.
Suddenly I come to the realization of what I should have done long before.

Slipping from my bed, I bend down on my knees.
I bow my head, fold my hands and pray to God, asking him to remove these concerns once and for all.

I feel a calming sense of release, no longer hearing the voice of worry telling me I must find a solution to my problem. All is quiet.

I wonder why it took me so long to give my problem over to God. Was it stubborn pride that made me feel I had to fix this on my own.

Once again I am reminded of the freeing power of God's grace when I've reached the end of all I can do.

I thank Him as I close my eyes, now realizing this had been in His hands all along. He was simply waiting for me to ask for his help.

In the stillness of the night I close my eyes and drift into a peaceful rest.

# You Honestly Know Me



With knowledge of…

The person I would become, my likes and dislikes, my human characteristics and personality traits.

You have provided…

The family I am a part of, the lasting friendships I have made along life's journey. The love we share for one another.

You have given me…

The man I fell in love with, the children we enjoy, the trials we face, the blessings we are showered with, the fun we share together.

You know…

My shortcomings as well as my strengths. My pleasures and displeasures. My tendencies.

You allow me…

The ability to make choices. To help others or turn away, to seek riches or be content, to accept You or deny You.

You…

Are always here for me, never sleeping, always listening.

Love me unconditionally, now and forever. Never judging, ever forgiving…

With You…

I am home, wherever life may lead me.

You honestly know me.

# Night Sounds

*I am awakened by the roar of what sounds like a plane flying overhead. The sound lasts much longer than usual, prompting many questionable thoughts in my mind.*

I wonder if it could be a train but dismiss the thought as it does not have the usual chugging sound.

The sound is louder than normal and I wonder why a plane would be flying so low. I consider getting up to look outside but decide whatever it is will be gone by the time I get to a window. I choose to lay still and listen...

A recent television series enters my mind and I imagine what it must have been like when the sound of such an overhead roar brought dread in knowing explosions would directly follow...

I think of those who sat in darkness, blinds drawn, praying they would not be seen by invading forces...

I cannot imagine what it must have been like to have lost loved ones and to have known such devastation.

I think of the world today and wonder what lies ahead...

Political unrest in a divided Nation...

Riots erupting across our nation through the incitement of racial exploitation...

Police officer's lives in grave danger as they are ordered to stand down...

Crime that runs rampant in our streets while violators walk free...

The virus, wondering how much longer we can endure it or abide by the restrictions that surround it...

My thoughts are interrupted by the warmth of my husband's body lying next to mine. His breathing is steady as he sleeps peacefully. I feel a sense of calm in knowing I need not worry.

I think of all I have to be thankful for. I feel the strength of God's loving arms surrounding not only myself, but my family and loved ones as well.

Should disaster strike, I will choose to put my trust in God.

I am confident God is our shield in whom we will find protection. He is our peace in whom we will find rest.

# Blessed

I awaken to a recurring pain in my foot and know
something is not right.

Looking down I see its purple color. This in itself is alarming but I keep silent.

I have just suffered through a shoulder surgery, followed by a season of Covid.

I cannot allow my body to be once again stricken with yet another problem, so I suffer through the pain.

My husband asks to see my foot and is alarmed. I am once again admitted to the hospital; this time with a blood clot.

It is a miracle I did not lose my foot as the blood clot is removed. I am being monitored for further developments as I return home.

Through it all I realize how truly loved I am. God is but a breath away as he watches over me.

I am blessed beyond all measure.

*This was written for a dear friend who had a blot clot in her leg.*

# The Still Small Voice



Sometimes it is but a soft whisper and other times a sense that leaves me frozen in my steps.

I am learning to trust it as I am convinced it is God's way of protecting me. Not only from immediate danger, but heartache and blunders as well.

It can come in the form of a passing thought or in words audibly spoken by another.

It can come as a simple awareness, which I have oftentimes mistakenly dismissed.

It can also come in the form of a "red flag," prompting my immediate attention; almost as if an intuition.

Whatever the means I do not discount it as I know it is for my good as well as the good of others.

I believe it is the still small voice of God reaching down from Heaven to guide me along life's journey.

# I Will



Listening to the voices that surround me I am filled with a
desire to help, but how, and in what capacity…I ask myself.

You are the answer to my dilemma as I set forth a plan of action. You are
the master planner; the one all knowing…

I will listen to your still, yet powerful voice.
I will expect to see answers that go beyond my wildest comprehension.
I will trust you!

Amen

# I Belong to You

*Your light fills me as I smile. My lips sings praises to you, yet I find myself doing the very things I do not want to do.*

I am as a flame blown every which way by the wind; sometimes with purpose and contentment; sometimes with worry and despair.

If only I could stand firm, knowing the full beauty of your being; the stillness of your very presence.
As a flame that does not flicker in the breeze.

Are my desires so meaningless I effortlessly lay waste to them or am I purely lacking discipline and self-control?

I will trust your word to light my path. I will hold firmly to your hand; not caring where the wind may blow. I will earnestly seek and find you with your help.

I belong to you.

# The Pain of Letting Go

*I wonder what it would have been like for Joseph
and Mary as parents…*

To see Jesus and his brother, James, play as children,
To wash their little hands and feet at the end of the day,
To see them giggle as they shared secrets together,
To tuck them into bed at night, after saying their prayers,
To hear them laugh and watch them grow up, loving them both dearly.

I think about…

The sadness they must have felt when Jesus left to do His
Father's work.
The rumors they must have heard as they prayed for His safety.
The excitement they must have felt when they knew He was close by.
The wonderment they must have had in hearing about the good He was
doing and the miracles He had performed.

It is hard to understand…

The painful rage that must have consumed them at seeing Him suffer as
he did.
The desperation of seeing Him nailed to a cross and watching Him die a
gruesome death.
The tears they must have cried as they begged God to spare his life.
The questions they must have had.

They understood…

His relationship with God Almighty.
The precious gift they had been given.

How hard it was to let go.

They saw…

His triumphant resurrection over death.
God's promises fulfilled for all mankind through…
Jesus.

# Why?



Not able to comprehend
Unless
One lives through it,
Or dies…

Was it a longing to be
Heard
A feeling of defeat,
Or more…

Were there signs of
Pulling away
From those who cared,
We wonder…

Was Loneliness the
Cause
Was pain the enemy,
Or both…

We pray…

# No Matter What



Sometimes I feel like I'm fighting a one man battle, yet I cannot let go. This is when I can trust God for the assurance of his Holy Spirit to lead me.

It could be the lost and helpless feeling of a family member who is sick, as I wait for answers. It could be concern over a loved one's safety or well-being.

It could be our country pulling away from its moral and spiritual values upon which it was built and seeing its destruction as it is literally taking place.

Whatever the cause, it can leave us with a hopeless feeling. But prayer changes things and GOD is good. He can fill us with peace in the midst of a storm.

I will place my trust in Him, even when I do not feel His presence, knowing He is but a heartbeat away, watching and waiting to see what I will do. Knowing He loves me.

If I fall He will catch me. If I take a wrong turn he will point me in the right direction. If I pray to Him He will hear me. If I mess up he will forgive me.

*No matter what…*

# Confident in Him

*Scattered thoughts spin through my mind; I try to focus on but one. I cannot seem to think anything through in its entirety, although I try.*

All avenues seem to lead to a large roundabout with passages veering off in many directions; thinking about the best route to safely exit.

Considering the courses we must take, anticipating both jubilation and success. Looking for the good each step will bring in our lives.

Excitement stirs within my soul with the expectation of new beginnings. Curiosity peeks my interest as we step out to explore new possibilities.

Wondering what new developments each morning will bring; each sunset will reveal. We have a heightened sense of calm in a sea of turbulent waters.

Watching life move swiftly around us, seeing changes, unbeknownst to us, yet somehow familiar; anticipating an air of peace in a time of uncertainty.

Trusting God that everything will work according to His perfect plan; praying all will come together beautifully in the end; confident He is in control.

# A Mother's Love

*A mother's love goes deeper than words.*

A mother's love is one that would rather suffer, than see her own children suffer.

A mother's love is unconditional, yet firm. It is sometimes overwhelming, but not with ill intent.

A mother's love would fight to save her children.

A mother's love celebrates her children's achievements.

A mother's love is not fickle; nor does it change with the wind. It is consistent and reliable.

A mother's love is one that cries' with her children when their hearts are broken and holds their hands when they are sick.

A mother's love is one that prays for her children, always thankful for answered prayers.

A mother's love is one which believes the best in her children, standing by them through thick and thin.

A mother's love enjoys the companionship of her children; always looking forward to their next visit.

A mother's love is a love that lasts a lifetime and forever...

# Actions Speak

*It is our privilege and honor as a born again believer in Jesus Christ to be acceptable of others, whether we approve of their lifestyle or not.*

Fully aware of our own weaknesses, we are to be strong in Christ; not to be confused with overbearing, intolerable or judgmental.

We are human and subject to human failings. We do not sit in a judgement seat, nor would we want to, lest we be judged ourselves.

It is not our job to criticize; but rather to build up, encourage and assist.

We are to live in unity; having our own set of values, while at the same time, appreciating the values and sensitivities of others.

Helping the weak, assisting the strong, encouraging the timid; while standing up for what and who we believe in.

Strength comes through believing. Belief comes through trusting. Trust comes through faith in God's living word.

Our actions speak louder than words.

# And I Believe



Life's many pleasures,
the best life can offer. All is unclear.

Trusting in God I see...

His many pleasures, prayers being answered, and I believe.

Yet ...

Who knows the answers to where we are going, what we are here for,
what is our purpose.

And I am I sure...

God is our anchor, author, perfector,
his way is better...

And I believe.

# And You Wait

*Watching a loved one who is
struggling is very hard to do.*

Wishing you could wind back time to a healthier place; a happier place, but you cannot.

And you wait…

Offering comfort and care the best you know how; hoping it will somehow speed up the process but some things just have to run their own course.

And you wait…

Praying for relief and comfort; asking for a quick recovery; knowing your prayers will be answered when the timing is right.

And you wait…

# Bite Your Tongue



When red flags rise within one's mind and the temptation to lash out and set another straight is almost suffocating, it is imperative to stop and think about what we are about to say. In other words, "bite our tongue."

We must consider the following. Could our outburst be damaging to another's sense of self-worth? Will it cause an underlying current of anger and resentment? Is it only to satisfy our own pride or is it truly justifiable and necessary?

These are questions I must ask myself. I am not a hot-headed person and am not easily angered or agitated, but I do have a limit and have found myself in this predicament from time to time with an immediate desire to speak my mind.

I have lashed out, only to have felt regret, wishing I had kept quiet. I have also stopped and considered my options, for which I have been thankful. Words spoken in anger can be hurtful beyond repair, as they can never be taken back.

I admire a person with self-control; one not easily provoked with a calmness about them. One who takes the time to cool off when agitated and handles a situation in a skillful manner. This is who I want to be.

A person who cannot control their tongue is a difficult person to associate with. They could potentially put themselves and others in a dangerous situation. They can become hardened and opinionated. Their words can cripple and defame another.

Through it all I have come to the conclusion it is a good thing to "bite one's tongue," cool off and think things through. Better to simmer in silence alone, than open a "can of worms," that can never be closed.

# Gods Masterpiece

*The glistening dew*
*Lends sparkle to the artist's*
*Rendition of light.*

When God created morning dew
He knew it would be the perfect ingredient
In His already perfect masterpiece.

# Gossip

> *Twisted, ugly strands of morbid slander,*
> *accompanied by gut wrenching pangs of endless*
> *guilt.*

To feel this single thread of selfish satisfaction is but a fleeting moment in the prison of regret.

Take the road less traveled to the highway of forgiveness where peace abides.

To enter the arena of self-satisfaction at the expense of another is poison to one's soul.

# Imagine

*Our senses are something that could easily be taken for granted, until we were to suddenly lose them.*

Without taste food would become an essential tool of survival, no longer enjoyed but rather, tolerated.

Voices we have known and loved would be silent. Noises we have shut out would be a blessing to hear just one more time.

No longer could we savor the aroma of a home cooked meal or enjoy the smell of freshly cut grass.

Gone would be our ability to feel, no longer being able to distinguish hot from cold; sharp from soft.

Loss of eyesight would be the most devastating, leaving us in a world of total darkness.

Imagine losing them all at once; no smells to entice us, no sounds to direct us, no sense of touch, no sense of taste, while at the same time being trapped in a world of darkness.

We would be as an empty shell.

Thank God for our senses.

# Motherhood

*Movement stirs within the body of a young woman. A sometimes gentle movement, other times a mighty kick.*

The movement is observed with a smile; a sign of a healthy child waiting to make their much anticipated entrance into this world.

To experience the miracle of new life within one's self is mesmerizing; spectacular in and of itself. A bond like no other as infant and mother connect.

The mother does all she can to protect this gentle treasure. She is beautifully talented in understanding the needs of her unborn child.

She will be a loving mother. The baby will be treasured and adored by all. The amazing miracle of birth!

# Simply Trust Him

> *When life suffocates us, entangling us in its twisted
> arms of restless despair…*

Simply trust Him.

When wakeful moments lead to sleepless nights of worry and anxious thoughts…

Simply trust Him.

When fear grips us, threatening our self-reliance and our ability to protect ourselves…

Simply trust Him.

When loneliness weighs us down and those we love are far away…

Simply trust Him.

As we seek the love and power of God himself…

Simply trust Him.

# Trust Him

*I feel good today, I hear our son say after weeks of
feeling under the weather.*

My head and back do not hurt, I hear my mother say after a bad fall.

The inflammation has left my body, I hear myself say to my husband.

She has finally been able to see the right doctor, I hear a friend say in a text.

These are just a few of the many answered prayers I have been made aware of in just one day.

Surely if I fine tune my ears to listen more intently; my eyes to see more clearly; my heart to care more deeply, I will learn of many more.

Surrounded by Gods healing grace, we are not alone in our sufferings. He hears our pleas for help and touches us with healing power.

The answer lies in Trusting Him

# Seasons of Life

*I have found life to be a series of meaningful events,*
*each centered around a particular season of life.*

My early years brought wonder and learning.

Through teenage years I experienced the excitement of choosing ones goals, friendship and dating.

As a young woman I found true love,
enjoying the blessings of marrying my best friend, and found happiness in becoming a mother.

As a couple we experienced companionship and hard work, while enjoying each other and the fruits of our labor.

As parents we watched our children grow, loved them, and did our best to prepare them for life's challenges.

With siblings we shared good times, enjoying one another as time would allow, looking forward to our next reunion.

As adults we enjoyed our parents. We laughed with them and cried with them; doing our best to be there when they needed a friend.

Today our love grows deeper yet for one another. We value friendships and time spent with family. We plan for retirement.

Our next season of life has begun with new challenges and blessings we will meet. We pray for our children, loved ones and country.

Although separated by distance we will remain close. Through the strength of God's grace we will be strong.

# Behold I Stand at the Door and Knock



Yet it comes
Whether a pounding rap or delicate tap; I am too busy to be bothered...

Yet it comes
Something important is in the making and I am preoccupied...

Yet it comes
Trying to sleep, I wonder why I must be bothered by this continual knocking ...

Yet it comes
Persistent and never failing, I am now too tired to open the door...

Yet it comes
On my knees and praying diligently, I search for answers...

Yet it comes
Finally unable to ignore it any longer I concede...

And I stare

Before me stands my Lord and Savior...

I am loved

*Based on Revelation 3:20*

Kerry was born in Fremont, Michigan and is happily married to the love of her life.

She enjoys spending quality time with her family and friends.

In addition to this book, Kerry and her daughter Sarah, have edited and revised several of her children's books, with their first of three being, "I'd Rather Eat Worms!"

Two of their children's books are written under the pen name, Grandma Batchie. They include, "A Box of Socks," and "The Vox... a new broom for Hilda."

All of their children's books are safe reading material for children. All promote being kind to one another, sharing with others and standing up for one's self and others, by not following the crowd.

Kerry has also recently completed a three book psychological crime series entitled, "The Undoing of Kelly Thomas."